Viv e Allen B/day 93

# WESTERN STEAM IN COLOUR

# BRANCH LINES

## Chris Leigh

First published 1992

ISBN 0 7110 2036 1

**Terminal House Shepperton TW17 8AS**
Telephone: Walton-on-Thames (0932) 228950
Fax: 0932 232366 Telex: 929806 IALLAN G
Registered Office: Terminal House, Shepperton TW17 8AS
Phototypeset and Printed by Ian Allan Printing at their works at Coombelands in Runnymede, England

*Front cover:*
Tavistock South was the main intermediate station on the rambling branch round Dartmoor from Plymouth to Launceston. The station here boasted a Brunelian train shed under which broad gauge dimensions allowed for three standard gauge tracks. The light and agile Churchward Prairie tanks of the '45xx' and '4575' classes were mainstay of this line and many other West Country branches with weight restrictions. One of the later series, No 5541, of Plymouth Laira depot, waits with a southbound train on 2 May 1961. Laira's 83D shed code also covered the sub-shed at Launceston where this locomotive would probably have been based. *R. C. Riley*

*Right:*
The Severn Valley and Much Wenlock lines bisected the very cradle of the industrial revolution, passing close to the Coalbrookdale Ironworks, where the parts for Abraham Darby's iron bridge had been cast in 1777. The Ironworks clock tower stands in the centre of this view and the area today forms part of Ironbridge Gorge Museum. Unusual motive power for the 4.40pm Wellington-Much Wenlock service is provided by Ivatt '2MT' 2-6-2T No 41201, seen coming off Coalbrookdale viaduct on 9 June. *M. Mensing*

***Dedication***
*To the memory of Tom Bye and Alice Tucker, Station Master and Lady Porter at Staines West, and the staff of countless other WR branch lines who made them the much-loved institution that they were.*

# Introduction

The Great Western branch line was probably the best loved of all our railway institutions, Many authors and railway enthusiasts have tried to explain the mysterious fascination which the rural branch lines of the Western held for their devotees. I would not wish to try and define the reasons why we loved them. It is sufficient to know that we did, and that we enjoyed them as a hobby interest for which they were never intended, while most of them made little or no profit for the promoters who built them with the intention of making their fortune.

Those which had independent beginnings seldom took very long to fall into the hands of their big neighbour, the Great Western. Indeed, many were operated by the GWR from the outset. That company also promoted a number of feeder lines for its own system, so by the dying years of the Victorian era the GWR's Paddington-Bristol 'trunk' had developed to a network of main lines radiating to the West of England, South Wales and the Midlands, intersected by secondary mainlines and with branches penetrating into the voids between them.

In the more rural areas some of these lines experienced problems of viability from the early years of the present century and the GWR came up with developments such as railmotors and new unstaffed halts, designed to cut costs and encourage traffic. Despite the onset of decline, very few saw closure until after World War 2 when road competition and rapidly rising costs really began to make an impact. Reduction of costs by reducing staff and introducing diesel traction did not prove to be their salvation and with the Beeching Report of 1963 most of the Western branches which had not already succumbed, bowed to the inevitable and were closed.

There have been many books about GWR branch lines, either in general or covering a specific line in great detail. Very few have included any significant colour content. As a lover of Western branch lines, two of the earliest volumes in my collection were the *GWR Branch Line Albums.* It was a chance conversation which led me to suggest that Ian Allan should attempt to do a branch line album in colour. Perhaps it was inevitable, having put forward the idea, that I should be asked to produce it, but it did pose a problem because I had no suitable colour photographs of my own.

Born too late to know most of these branches in the steam era, my meagre photographic efforts had been concentrated on recording mainly dieselised or closed and derelict stations on the rather unstable colour print stock of the mid-1960s.With the availability of GWR diesel railcars from the 1930s, and BR vehicles from 1958 onwards, many branches saw quite early dieselisation, while colour transparency film was not being widely used by railway photographers till much later in the 1960s. Only one or two enlightened souls filled their cameras with the slow colour films of the day and took publishable colour material in the 1950s.

At first I was not at all sure that there would be sufficient available material to produce a book. Approaches to some well-known photographers soon proved my fears unfounded and what materialised in the post was a variety of interesting material. From the outset I had decided to incorporate early diesel scenes if they were interesting and covered locations that were otherwise unobtainable. I also wanted views which showed a lot more than just a branch line train. I wanted stations and infrastructure, and all the paraphernalia of the traditional branch line scene. I certainly got that, but I also received some marvellous scenic shots and it soon became apparent that this could be the *prettiest* colour book published so far. If you enjoy mellowed buildings, platform gardens with roses, and trains ambling through glorious England, I think you will appreciate much of what is in these pages. If you also enjoyed the more esoteric surroundings of dilapidated stations visited by the once-weekly goods or enlivened briefly by an enthusiasts railtour, you should be well pleased too.

I enjoyed all this, and it was marvellous to have my memories reinvigorated by pictures in colour. Most are of the very best quality.

I rejected many which were delightful, largely due to shortage of space, and the elimination was based on technical quality (sharpness, exposure, colour defects caused by ageing). I tried for as broad a geographical spread as possible and for as much variety in motive power as I could find and in order to show the whole branch line picture there is a smattering of diesels, DMUs, and the occasional train-less view. Thus we have a Dean goods, an outside cylinder saddle tank, a 'Hall' and a Southern Mogul among the staple diet of Prairies and Panniers. Among the DMUs are four-wheel railbuses and an 0-6-0 shunter. Of course I ended up with too many and the weeding out process became protracted. Finally, I chose mainly those where the sun was shining. After all, in those happy days of our memory, the sun was always shining, wasn't it?

**Chris Leigh** **Old Windsor 1991**


**Acknowledgements**

This book would not have been possible but for the willingness of a number of excellent photographers to loan their valuable originals. Grateful thanks are expressed to the following: B. J. Ashworth, Hugh Ballantyne, Ron White (Colour-Rail), D. Eade, Michael Farr, The late R. M. S. Hall, Dr K. A. Jaggers, M. Mensing, Bill Potter, Dick Riley, A. L. Ross, E. G. Sambrook, James Tawse, Bob Treacher, Peter Treloar and Dr M. H. Yardley.


**Note**

The illustrations are arranged in approximately geographical order, outwards from London, except where it has been necessary to group pictures together because of a similar theme or because of colour quality considerations due to the use of varying original film-stocks.

*Below:*
The Great Western made much of its main line to Torbay, serving Torquay, Paignton and Kingswear where a railway-owned ferry conveyed passengers across the River Dart to Dartmouth. Only in BR days was the route run down to the point where the Paignton-Kingswear section faced closure and was purchased by a private operator. Between Paignton and Kingswear the main intermediate station was Churston and from a bay platform here an auto-train worked the short branch to Brixham. Opened in 1868 at the whim of a local landowner, the branch in fact developed a healthy fish traffic, Brixham having one of the principal fishing fleets in the southwest. The branch closed in May 1963, by which time the service had been dieselised with a Gloucester single unit railcar. This view shows the station, high above Brixham harbour, with No 1452 coupled chimney-first to its auto-trailer, on 6 June 1959. *W. Potter*

# London area

*Right:*
Though their beginnings had been much the same as other WR branches, the branch lines close to London had developed a more urban character by the 1960s. Closest in were the Brentford branch, which had closed to passengers in 1942, and that to Greenford from West Ealing. The Brentford branch had remained in use for goods, and the northern section between Southall and the Great West Road continues in the same use today. In the 1960s the line still crossed the Great West Road by a substantial girder bridge, but its best known feature has always been Windmill Bridge or the so-called 'three bridges' at Southall, where road crosses over canal aqueduct over railway. This is the view from that bridge on 25 July 1965 as '57xx' 0-6-0PT No 9773 of Southall shed takes the 'Thames Valley Railtour' down to Brentford. *T. B. Owen*

*Far right:*
Two branches diverged from the main line just west of West Drayton station. The line to Uxbridge Vine Street curved away northwards and almost immediately another line split from it and turned southwards underneath the main line to skirt west of Heathrow Airport to Colnbrook and Staines West. It had opened in 1885 largely as a result of Staines people being dissatisfied with the service they received from the LSWR. South of Colnbrook the branch crossed Staines Moor and remained rural in character through to the terminus. Goods services on the southern section ceased in the mid-1950s, but with passenger service withdrawal imminent, an oil depot was opened on the site of the goods yard at Staines West in 1964. The last passenger service operated on 27 March 1965 but oil trains ran until the M25 motorway obliterated the route in 1981. Staines West station was converted from a private house and is seen here with Pressed Steel railcar No W55028 forming the 11.30am to West Drayton on 30 January 1965. In the background the flag on the brewery tower flies at half-mast for the funeral of Sir Winston Churchill. *Hugh Ballantyne*

2A82

*Above:*
In the years following closure to passenger services, there were few special trains to visit Staines West. The first, and as it transpired the only steam working, was an occasion not to be missed. Staines West was within walking distance of home, so despite a severe asthma attack I walked there with my camera on 25 July 1965 to record '57xx' 0-6-0PT No 9773 arriving with an REC/LCGB branch line tour. Unfortunately the shutter mechanism jammed and I got only a roll of blank film for my trouble. Fortunately, others had more luck. No 9773 is seen here passing Colnbrook Estate Halt on the down journey. This concrete halt, seen to the left of the last coach, was erected in 1961 to serve local factories and closed when passenger services finished in March 1965. The train had started from Kensington Olympia and was formed of SR corridor stock. Perhaps the most interesting feature of this view lies between the rails ahead of the train. After the branch closed, BR experimented with inductive train control – 'driverless trains' – controlled by a zig-zag wire laid between the running rails. A specially-equipped platelayers' trolley was used for the trials, but local legend suggests that major problems occurred because 'totters' tore up the wire as fast as BR could lay it! *T. B. Owen*

*Right:*
I trust readers will permit me the indulgence of using what I consider to be a perfect view of the perfect branch line train on my home route, even if it is a diesel. Services to Staines West finished on 27 March 1965 and were operated by a three-car unit, so this view on the previous day was the last day of operation by the customary Pressed Steel single-unit railcar. No W55022 is seen calling at Colnbrook with a down working and 27 years later this railcar is still working in the area. It carries the full 'Staines West' in its destination blind (some cars just showed 'Staines' following the abortive proposal to divert trains into Staines Central (SR) station) and the correct '2A82' headcode for the Staines branch passenger train. The lady loading parcels appears to be Alice Tucker, the porteress from Staines West.
At Colnbrook the track, now disused, still crosses the Old Bath Road, but the station has completely vanished under the Murco terminal which receives aviation fuel for Heathrow and now brings Class 60 diesels to this spot. *T. B. Owen*

2A82
STAINES WEST

PARCELS OFFICE
1453

*Left:*
Though goods services to Staines West had ceased in the mid-1950s, and passenger services were to be withdrawn in 1965, complete closure of the branch was frustrated by the establishment of a small oil depot on the Staines West goods yard site in 1964. The depot was a distribution point for central heating fuel so traffic fluctuated with demand and was seldom sufficient to make rail traffic worthwhile. Nevertheless, in 1981 when the M25 motorway severed the route, it was found necessary to connect the depot to the SR so that service could continue. It lasted, in fact, until 24 June 1991 and as this is being written the *very* last train to Staines West has recently operated. The very first train into the depot on 19 June 1964 was the only steam-hauled one, subsequent workings passing to 'Hymek' diesels. Having parked the tanks in the depot, 2-6-2T No 6143 is about to return to West Drayton with the barrier wagons which were placed between locomotive and tanks to reduce the fire risk. *K. A. Jaggers*

*Below left:*
The line between Maidenhead and High Wycombe, built as the Wycombe Railway, became a minor diversionary route with the advent of the Birmingham direct line between High Wycombe and London. A short branch along the Thames riverbank from Marlow joined the Wycombe Railway at Bourne End, with a north-facing junction. Today the line between Bourne End and Wycombe has gone, and trains still operate from Maidenhead to Marlow, reversing at Bourne End. Sadly, Marlow station site has been completely redeveloped and the station there is just a short, bare platform. This view is a poignant reminder of what has been lost. The 'Marlow Donkey', No 1453 and a single BR autotrailer of the *Wren* type, stand at Marlow on 30 April 1960. A bicycle is being off-loaded and what appears to be part of the station furniture stands on the platform ready to be placed aboard. After dieselisation, steam re-appeared on the branch for a weekend in 1973 to mark the line's centenary. *T. B. Owen*

*Right:*
The branch to the important river resort of Henley-on-Thames diverges from the mainline immediately west of Twyford station, where the up-side platform is provided with a bay for the branch trains. This was always one of the busier branches between Reading and London and though it has been heavily rationalised over recent years, it shares, with the Windsor branch, the distinction of never having had to fight off closure proposals. The two intermediate stations, Wargrave and Shiplake, are nowadays unstaffed, but once boasted attractive GWR structures. The branch was double-track and saw some through services to and from Paddington worked by 4-6-0s. Here, a Henley-Twyford local is entering Shiplake, formed of a couple of suburban coaches headed by '57xx' 0-6-0PT No 4609. The footbridge served a small level crossing and provided access to the island platform. *Colour-Rail*

*Above:*
Wargrave station suffered progressive reduction from two platforms to one, then becoming unstaffed and eventually suffering the loss of its station building too. In happier times this typical Thames Valley station basked in summer sun as '14xx' 0-4-2T No 1444 called with a Henley-Twyford autotrain on 3 March 1958. The locomotive is in lined green, but with the earlier BR emblem, while the autotrailer is a converted steam railmotor car nearing the end of its 50-year service life. The footbridge, station building, sheds, seat, shaded gas lamp and nameboard are all pure GWR although the nameboard is painted black in GWR style, rather than the brown and cream usually associated with the Western Region. A number of WR stations on the London Division received black and white signware around this time. *T. B. Owen*

*Right:*
Most of the Thames Valley branches could boast at least one weekday through service to Paddington for what have since become known as 'Commuters'. Dieselisation saw most of these services turned over to DMU formations, though fast peak-hour main line services to junction stations such as Maidenhead and Twyford continued to boast locomotive haulage. Steam working to Henley brought 4-6-0s and could even see a 'Castle' working through on what was then a double track branch. Running on immaculately maintained track, a smart 'Hall' 4-6-0 No 6913 *Levens Hall* heads the 7.48am Henley-Paddington near Wargrave. The splendid white exhaust against a blue sky shows that the morning of 17 March 1961 heralded a beautiful crisp spring day. *Gerald T. Robinson*

6913

*Left:*
It was the East Gloucestershire Railway's station at Fairford which first aroused my interest in GWR stations. Quite by chance we stopped there one day whilst looking for a picnic spot on a journey home from holiday. The station was closed and derelict, but still full of interest. All the EGR stations were built to a similar design and all but Alvescot were built of local stone. In the twilight years of the Great Western branch line there was something magical and exciting about the walk down an approach road to a rural station. Warm sunshine, flower-beds, weedy sidings hiding all sorts of delights, and a tremendous air of anticipation. Actually arriving on the platform and watching the train arrive was, to me, even better than the train ride! Some of that magic is conveyed by this view of Lechlade station from the approach road. It is marvellous, even without a train in sight, and I could not resist including it in this volume, for that reason. The date was 2 September 1959, a couple of years before closure. *E. G. Sambrook*

*Above:*
The Banbury and Cheltenham Railway was built as a through route across GWR territory, but it really came to nothing and was eventually absorbed by the GWR, becoming just another sleepy rural line. Between Kingham and Banbury all its stations were similar in style, and Hook Norton is a good example. The section between Kings Sutton and Chipping Norton, including Adderbury, Bloxham and Hook Norton stations, closed in 1952, but the Railway Enthusiasts Club managed a railtour over the closed section on 14 September 1963. Suburban '61xx' 2-6-2T No 6111 is wearing express headlamps for the occasion. Note the old-style wooden token catcher post on the right, newer ones had metal posts and a net behind the hook. *Colour-Rail*

1658

R.E.C.
1365

*Left:*
December 1951 had seen the Berkshire branch line between Uffington and Faringdon closed to passenger traffic, but goods workings remained to attract the enthusiast, infrequent though they were. On 13 May 1961 enthusiasts were able to imitate the branch goods by travelling down to Faringdon on a brake van tour. No 1658 was one of a class of lightweight 0-6-0PTs designed by Hawksworth for weight-restricted branch lines, and built after Nationalisation. They were not auto-fitted and generally were restricted to shunting and branch freight work. Also of interest is the bauxite-painted 'Toad' brake van, one of the vacuum-braked examples, less common than the unfitted, grey-painted version of the standard GWR 20ton goods brake. The stone-built locomotive shed can be seen on the left, and the goods shed to the right of the single platform. *R. C. Riley*

*Below left:*
Enthusiasts had an opportunity to travel down to Faringdon on a special chartered by the Railway Enthusiasts Club of Farnborough on 26 April 1959. This was made into an even more exciting opportunity by the choice of motive power brought up to the Thames Valley specially for the occasion. There were just two of Churchward's 1910-built 0-6-0STs left in traffic doing the work for which they had been built, dock shunting at Weymouth and Plymouth. In this view No 1365 has run round its two-coach 'B-set' and stands at Faringdon waiting to return to the main line at Uffington. Behind it can be glimpsed the curious twin hipped roofs of the little stone station building, together with a concrete provender store of postwar construction, a common feature of rural stations throughout BR. *R. C. Riley*

*Right:*
Branches which had closed to passengers, but remained in place for occasional goods trains, were most attractive to the railway enthusiasts of the 1950s and 1960s, and many railtours were devised to include such lines on their itinerary. The old tramway from Moreton-in-Marsh to Shipston-on-Stour had closed as long ago as July 1929, but it was the high-spot of a tour on 17 April 1955 which provides the opportunity to include another charismatic GWR locomotive class, the Dean goods 0-6-0. Reading-based No 2474 is seen at the newly-ballasted Shipston terminus with four carmine and cream coaches including at least one ex-LMS brake second. *R. C. Riley*

# Swindon area branches

*Below:*
The branch line from Swindon to Highworth, closed to passengers in March 1963, diverged from the main line through yards and factories east of the station and was scarcely noticeable to the passing traveller. It served several villages which formed dormitory areas on the outskirts of Swindon and remained in use by workmen's trains serving Swindon Works and the Pressed Steel car body plant for many years after passenger traffic ceased. It was restricted to use by the lightest locomotives and on 13 May 1961, when an enthusiasts' brake van tour visited the line, the little '16xx' 0-6-0PT No 1658 was provided. It is here seen at Highworth where the delightful timber station would make a perfect model, complete with period-piece Austin A55 Cambridge parked outside. *R. C. Riley*

*Right:*
The Tetbury branch, 7miles 19chains in length, from Kemble on the Swindon-Gloucester main line was opened in 1889. Another delightful rural Great Western branch, halts were provided at Jackaments Bottom, Rodmarton and a more substantial timber station at Culkerton. Tetbury originally had a timber station building but in 1916 the GWR replaced this with its standard red brick pattern, though interestingly re-using window frames and awning from the original. Light axle-loadings on the line restricted the locomotives to '16xx', '74xx', and '57xx' 0-6-0PTs, '45xx' 2-6-2Ts and the customary 0-4-2Ts. Some mixed trains were run with unfitted wagons and non-auto 0-4-2Ts of the '58xx' series were frequently used. Auto-trains were less usual, but on 5 April 1964, the Sunday after the last passenger train had run, the Gloucestershire Railway Society mustered '14xx' 0-4-2T No 1472 and a couple of trailers for a railtour, seen here waiting to return, engine-first, to Kemble. *W. Potter*

1472
GLOUCESTERSHIRE
RAILWAY
SOCIETY

*Above:*
This delightful portrait taken from the cattle dock, shows Tetbury station, looking towards the stop-blocks on 4 May 1963. On the right is the station building with one of the AC Cars four-wheel rail-buses waiting in the platform. On the left are the locomotive facilities, although by this time the shed was used only for overnight stabling of the railbus. The coal on the timber stage is probably superfluous, as only the branch goods was steam-worked at this time and the locomotive would have been adequately coaled at Swindon. All steam workings ceased only a couple of months after this picture was taken. Though the engine shed dated from 1889, the raised tank on the rear was a later addition. A carefully parked locomotive inside the shed would prevent the tank from freezing. *W. Potter*

*Right:*
The GRS railtour of 5 April 1964 is here seen at Cirencester Town station, terminus of the other branch from Kemble, and which had also closed to passengers on the previous day. This station was once terminus of the line from Swindon before completion through to Gloucester left it on a branch. As befitted its status, the Brunel building once had a trainshed, but this had been removed many years earlier, and the station received a degree of 'modernisation' in the late 1950s. Here, we can see that the GRS special is formed of two of the 1951-built 'Hawksworth' auto-trailers, in the final lined maroon livery. Though several of these coaches survive in preservation, none is in authentic condition, their owners preferring bogus GWR livery.
*W. Potter*

1472

*Below:*
A splendid portrait of old and new side by side, as the GRS railtour poses with AC Cars railbus No W79977 at Cirencester, with the standard GWR signalbox on the left, and an interesting goods yard hand crane to the right. No W79977 was damaged in a shunting accident at Swindon and so became the only member of the class to receive the later style DMU livery of dark green with yellow warning panels. It is interesting to speculate how it came to be at Cirencester the day after passenger services ceased. Surely there would have been little point in publicising the vehicle at this stage, so it seems unlikely it was brought down specially for the occasion. Perhaps it had been stabled at Cirencester overnight and posed for this picture before its final return to Swindon. In any event it was subsequently banished to the depths of Cornwall to see out its short working life on the Bodmin North branch of the former Southern Region. *W. Potter*

*Right:*
One line has to be included in this volume as an 'honorary' branch line because it had all the desirable branchline features – pretty stations and halts, fine scenery and archetypal auto-train services. The Golden Valley, from Sapperton down to the outskirts of Gloucester remains one of the Western's most attractive rail routes, but until 1965 was the stronghold of the last regular auto-train workings on the WR with a handful of '14xx' class 0-4-2Ts retained to work with BR-built trailers. One of the regulars was No 1451, here seen at Stroud taking water ready for the run up Sapperton bank to Chalford with the 1.03pm from Gloucester on 26 March 1964. Scarcely a trace of Chalford or Brimscombe stations or the intermediate halts now survives, but the gated crossing and signalbox at St Mary's, near Brimscombe, are something of a time-warp. *Hugh Ballantyne*

1451

GENTLEMEN
CHALFORD
1409

*Left:*
The previous caption mentioned the Golden Valley's pretty stations, and none was better than Chalford, seen here on 25 June 1962. The pristine platforms boasted doormats outside every door and gas-lighting remained on the platforms until closure in 1965. The red brick building on the up platform, seen here, is a standard GWR design with rounded blue bricks to all corners. Note the red and cream coach tucked away in the goods yard on the right. Auto-tank No 1409 is slipping quietly away from the down platform, propelling its trailer down Sapperton bank to Gloucester. *R. C. Riley*

*Below left:*
Chalford had no bay platform for the local trains from Gloucester. It was provided with a headshunt to enable the train to clear the main line to take water, and a refuge behind the up platform for longer layovers. Here, '14xx' 0-4-2T No 1451 has pulled forward into the headshunt to take water before crossing over to the down platform ready for the run back to Gloucester. This locomotive was a regular on the service until it closed on 2 November 1964. This is a June 1962 view.
*Derek Cross*

*Below:*
The branch line to Malmesbury in Wiltshire had the unusual distinction that its junction with the main line was actually moved to a different route. As built, the junction was at Dauntsey, on the main line between Swindon and Chippenham. When the direct South Wales line from Wootton Bassett opened in the early years of the present century, it crossed the branch near Kingsmead crossing, Little Somerford. From 1933 the GWR connected the branch to the South Wales line, with trains working to Malmesbury from Little Somerford, and the section to Dauntsey was dismantled. The remaining section closed to passengers in September 1951, but remained open for goods traffic. In the 1960s it was in use largely for movements of agricultural machinery and Swindon was in the habit of rostering its little 204hp 0-6-0 diesel shunters for trip workings over this line and the branches to Highworth and Chippenham-Calne. Malmesbury's delightful little stone terminus was reached through a tunnel under the hill on which the ruined abbey stands. No D2187 waits in the goods yard at Malmesbury with what must surely have been a lucrative load of farm machines on the daily freight service on 12 June 1962. *Hugh Ballantyne*

2B

*Left:*
The Calne branch boasted two intermediate halts in its 4.5mile length. First out of Chippenham was Stanley Bridge Halt, where a BRCW (Class 118) DMU is seen passing with a working from Calne in 1963. A variety of DMU types and the occasional steam-hauled train were provided by Bristol for this service, though once through workings beyond Chippenham ceased, the DMUs monopolised the branch. The halt served a few scattered farms but had enjoyed a substantial traffic in milk churns. These had necessitated the construction of a storage shed, known locally as 'the shed with the hole in the back'. It stood beyond the classic pagoda shelter provided for the passengers, but had been removed by the time of this view. Only the road overbridge survives at this spot. *Paul Strong/Colour-Rail*

*Below:*
In contrast to the typical GWR halt at Stanley Bridge, Black Dog Halt was far from a typical GWR halt. It was built as the private station for Bowood House, the nearby home of the Marquis of Lansdowne. He paid £55 for the construction of its timber 'shed' and refused to permit the erection of a nameboard, although the public were allowed to use the station. It passed to BR in 1952 and was painted in WR brown and cream and adorned with an enamelled metal plate bearing its name. In this view, looking towards Chippenham, the halt is seen from the loading bank which served the Estate's siding, in the foreground. There was no run-round loop and wagons were sometimes run out of the siding under gravity. Black Dog siding ground frame was housed in the little cream shed visible above the Bedford van which is parked on the approach road. The photographer's father was the last railwayman in charge of Black Dog and his appointment was required to have Lord Lansdowne's approval. *Don Lovelock*

*Below:*
The Midland & South Western Junction Railway was always a thorn in the flesh of the GWR. It cut across GWR territory from Andoversford, near Cheltenham, to Andover on the LSWR main line and provided a through route from the Midlands to Southampton. Thrust into the Great Western at the Grouping in 1923 it was always treated by its former enemy as a rural backwater, though it was to prove useful in World War 2 as it had done between 1914 and 1918. The GWR and later the Western Region rationalised the route and its services, through services gradually being replaced with a series of short local trains. The former MSWJR workshops at Cirencester Watermoor can be seen in the background of this view as '57xx' 0-6-0PT No 4697 arrives with the Sundays-excepted 6.07pm from Swindon Town on 23 May 1961. Damage to the underline bridge at the opposite end of the station had resulted in the passing loop through the platforms being lifted. Despite WR brown and cream paint, the seat and signalbox are unmistakeably MSWJR originals. *Hugh Ballantyne*

*Below:*
Looking towards Cheltenham on 18 August 1961 the camera shows the main platform at Cirencester Watermoor, trackless and in the last weeks of decline. '57xx' 0-6-0PT No 9773 (which receives a disproportionate amount of coverage in this volume) is about to depart with the 7.10pm Sundays-excepted to Swindon, conveying just one passenger! On the left are the water tank and a corrugated-iron bungalow which once served as a dwelling for a senior member of MSWJR staff. After the line closed its route through the ancient Roman town was largely obliterated and the station site redeveloped. *Hugh Ballantyne*

*Above:*
Last rites on the MSWJR were performed on 10 September 1961 with the running of a railtour over the entire route on behalf of the Stephenson Locomotive Society. Motive power was provided by 'Manor' class 4-6-0 No 7808 *Cookham Manor* which was turned at Ludgershall on the return trip, having to use outriggers because the turntable was too small. Here the southbound working is seen at Cricklade, north of Swindon. Note the outside-framed Siphon G, ex-works, in BR maroon livery with its louvres plated over, standing in the bay. Cricklade station stood derelict for several years after the line closed, before being completely redeveloped as a housing estate. *Hugh Ballantyne*

*Right:*
As a through route between Southern and Midland Regions, the ex-MSWJR line saw a fair variety of motive power, but in its twilight years the Southern moguls predominated. One of Maunsell's 'U' class 2-6-0s, rebuilt from 'River' class tanks, No 31795 bursts out of Chedworth tunnel with a southbound train on 22 March 1960. Due to the company's impecunious state, the line was built piecemeal, the northern section being the last to be completed. Indeed, the tunnel at Chedworth was the last major obstacle, work commencing in 1889 with the aid of mechanised excavating equipment. Even so, the through route did not open until 1891.
*B. J. Ashworth*

31795

1454

YATTON
JUNCTION FOR
CHEDDAR LINE AND
CLEVEDON

# West Country branches

*Left:*
Yatton station, between Bristol and Weston-super-Mare, was a major junction station, with the Cheddar Valley line from Witham coming in from the south and the short branch to Clevedon turning away to the north immediately beyond the platform end. Bristol Bath Road Depot's '14xx' 0-4-2T auto-tank No 1454 is attracting much attention from passengers off a main line train, no doubt a railtour, which stands at the adjacent platform. The little tank is being watered before taking its tatty 1951-built trailer in faded carmine livery down to the coast at Clevedon. Though both branches have gone, Yatton retains its fine Bristol & Exeter Railway station buildings, distinguished by having the various room designations, 'Booking Hall' and so on, carved in the stone lintels. *R. C. Riley*

*Bottom left:*
A view right across the western end of Yatton station, which shows the branch bay platforms for both the diverging lines. By this time, 17 August 1963, the Clevedon branch had been turned over to diesel multiple units, and a Derby three-car suburban set can be seen in the bay on the left. The main lines are empty, but '57xx' 0-6-0PT No 3702 is waiting, bunker first, with the 2.45pm to Witham over the Cheddar Valley line. On the right, a '2251' class 0-6-0 No 2268 is stabled. *Hugh Ballantyne*

*Right:*
Green-liveried '45xx' 2-6-2T No 4561 runs round its train at the south Devon branch terminus of Kingsbridge on 3 June 1961. It will then stable the carriages in the black corrugated iron carriage shed in the centre of the picture, which is partly obscured by the locomotive exhaust. This view of almost the whole station area shows a myriad tiny details. Note the bean sticks under the station nameboard. There is a concrete provender store (centre), a Morris Minor Post Office van loading mailbags on the station platform, and a locomotive coal wagon tucked away in the engine shed (right). The Brent-Kingsbridge branch closed in September 1963, by which time the passenger service had been dieselised with a single-unit railcar. *Peter W. Gray*

*Left:*
The starting signal at Gara Bridge is returning to 'danger' after the passing of '4575' 2-6-2T No 5533 with a train to Kingsbridge. Gara Bridge was the intermediate passing station on the Kingsbridge branch and boasted a level crossing and signalbox. The station building, set amid the rolling green Devon hills, was similar to others on the branch and built of local stone. The branch train is formed of a down-graded Collett corridor brake second and a much later 'suburban' non-corridor brake composite. Behind the train two green-painted camping coaches can be seen in the goods siding. Many redundant coaches were converted to self-catering holiday accommodation and placed at attractive locations for summer holiday letting, often to railway staff. *T B. Owen*

*Above:*
The lengthy cross-country line from Taunton to Barnstaple was probably one of the most scenic WR routes to be closed by Beeching, succumbing in October 1966. Once used to take Western through trains to Ilfracombe, it ran through deep wooded valleys and along the foothills of Exmoor. It was single track with some 10 intermediate stations at which trains could cross. Wiveliscombe was the last stop in Somerset and the section on to Venn Cross included the spectacular crossing of the Tone Valley on a high lattice girder viaduct. Typical of stations at the eastern end of the line, Wiveliscombe is seen here after closure. The single storey station building stands alongside the stone goods shed, and the platform-mounted signalbox is nearest the camera. *K. A. Jaggers*

1420

*Above left:*
The rural charm of WR branch lines was encapsulated in the 7.25mile branch from Tiverton Junction to Hemyock, though its beginnings were not strictly typical. It was one of the first lines to be built under the 1868 regulations which permitted economies of construction, in 'light railway' fashion, in return for restrictions in speed and axle-loading. The handicap of very sharp curves meant that special stock had to be provided when bogie coaches were introduced. The GWR used an ex-Barry Railway gas-lit vehicle, seen here, which BR eventually replaced with one of two Thompson coaches obtained from the Eastern Region. Dieselisation of passenger services was thus deferred and the '14xx' 0-4-2Ts monopolised passenger services until the end, although milk trains operated with NBL Type 2 diesels well into the 1970s. No 1420 heads the 1.40pm Tiverton Junction-Hemyock service away from Culmstock on 30 July 1959. *P. Q. Treloar*

*Left:*
The Culm Valley line's three stations, Uffculme, Culmstock and Hemyock, were all distinctive and followed the same basic design – a single platform with a small red brick building. At Uffculme on 15 June 1962, an immaculate '14xx' 0-4-2T No 1451 has arrived with a mixed train. The locomotive wears lined green BR livery with the final version of the lion-and-wheel crest and contrasts sharply with the tatty state of its carriage. The rest of the train comprises two BR bulk grain hoppers, a 16ton mineral wagon, a 12ton van and an ex-GWR 20ton 'Toad' brake van. The branch passenger services ceased from 9 September 1963, but milk trains continued into the 1970s. *R. C. Riley*

*Above:*
The other branch from Tiverton Junction was a very different affair, serving the important Devon market town of Tiverton, situated just off the main line. This line warranted a normal auto-train, usually comprising two trailers and a '14xx' tank known with great local pride as 'The Tivvy Bumper'. The ensemble is seen here leaving the terminus behind No 1451, with one of the 1951-built trailers at the rear. Tiverton station had been substantially modernised but was far larger than this simple service required. The standard GWR red brick signalbox stands on the right, but lifted tracks and stacked sleepers on the left signify that much of its usefulness had already gone by the time of this 1 July 1963 view. The branch eventually closed completely but one of the local engines, '14xx' 0-4-2T No 1442 was acquired for preservation on a plinth in the town. It has since been moved to form the centrepiece of a local museum. *R. C. Riley*

*Left:*
Closed to passengers in June 1958, the Teign Valley line between Exeter and Heathfield in South Devon, was severed east of Trusham in May 1961. One of many freight-only stubs which were left by service withdrawals at this time, it served a solitary customer with bulk powder 'Presflo' hopper wagons. On 10 August 1961 the dilapidated Trusham station is host to '57xx' 0-6-0PT No 3659 readying the thrice-weekly goods for return to Heathfield and, ultimately, Newton Abbot. *Hugh Ballantyne*

*Below:*
The branch to Moretonhampstead diverged from the Teign Valley line at Heathfield and the first station beyond the junction was Bovey, serving the town of Bovey Tracey. The passenger service between Newton Abbot and Moretonhampstead was withdrawn in June 1958, but a freight service remained to this point also at the time of our August 1967 visit. Among the wagons present was a tank privately owned by United Molasses, one of the freight customers at Bovey. The author's blue Hillman Minx can be seen beyond the station. It was much used for touring Western branch lines at this time.
*K. A. Jaggers*

*Above left:*
This fine view shows the terminus at Moretonhampstead with its timber-built Brunel trainshed and stone buildings. The goods shed has a substantial provender store built of corrugated iron, as was quite usual at rural stations. Such stores were usually provided for storage of farm feedstuffs delivered by rail in sacks and distributed to the farms by road. To judge from the sign on the goods shed, the whole structure was given over to this traffic, and the vacuum-fitted goods van coupled behind the locomotive also carries a farm supplier's label. The train is headed by a '41xx' 2-6-2T in the early-1950s unlined black livery and the carriages are two non-corridor Collett bow-ended vehicles, not one of the customary branch-line 'B' sets. The point in the foreground led to the engine shed, now the only structure left standing at this site. *Peter W. Gray*

*Left:*
The Plymouth-Launceston line was renowned for its glorious Devon scenery, which is shown at its best in this view of '4575' 2-6-2T No 5544 entering Liddaton Halt with a Launceston-bound working on 23 June 1962. The halt is of wooden construction and boasts a GWR-pattern nameboard and a rather spartan wooden shed for a shelter. The two-coach train is formed of an ex-LMS vehicle and a BR Mk1 brake second, the latter on menial duties for what was then a modern vehicle. Liddaton was on the northern section of the line and this view is looking back towards Lydford and Dartmoor. *R. C. Riley*

*Above:*
Between Tavistock and Lydford the GWR Launceston branch paralleled the Southern's Plymouth-Exeter main line and at Lydford they shared the same station, the GWR part, seen here, being built back to back with SR structures off the picture to the left. Though three members of staff can be seen, there are no passengers for the Launceston-bound train seen entering Lydford on 23 June 1962. The locomotive is '45xx' 2-6-2T No 4555, which was to become the first locomotive acquired for preservation by the Dart Valley Railway, some three years later. *R. C. Riley*

5569

*Left:*
A poem about the Plym valley line immortalised Yelverton's curious wooden station as 'most queer and polygonal'. In this view the five-sided building can be seen to the right of the train, with the remains of the former Princetown branch hidden behind it. The southbound train behind No 5569 of the ubiquitous small Prairies, is running wrong line, the other platform having been already taken out of use with final closure only some 18 months away. The last trains ran on 31 December 1962, the bitter weather and deep snow writing them into railway legend, as the last train did not actually reach 'home' until the following day. *R. C. Riley*

*Below:*
From Yelverton up to Princetown, high up on Dartmoor, the branch line wound a convoluted route around the hills, serving only some tiny villages and outposts of civilisation. Remote and desolate in bad weather, the Princetown branch looks benign enough in this view of a Yelverton-bound working stopping at Dousland on 5 July 1955. The locomotive is No 4410 one of the small class of '44xx' 2-6-2Ts built specially for light and steeply-graded branches.The old GWR coaches show how smart and attractive the carmine and cream livery could look when well kept, but sadly the locomotive is not in matching condition. *R. C. Riley*

*Left:*
The branch to Looe from Liskeard descends to Coombe Junction then takes its course along the bank of the East Looe river all the way to the delightful fishing village of Looe. The station faced the river and the line continued across the foot of the road bridge to a goods yard alongside the harbour. The L&LR station building was a distinctive, if not very beautiful, wooden structure. The small Prairies almost monopolised the branch because of their superior performance on the steep gradient up to Liskeard. No 5539 is seen bringing the coaches of the Liskeard train up from the quay sidings, which is where the run-round loop was situated, and scenes viewed in this direction are quite rare. Note the healthy traffic in fish, judging from the boxes on the platform in this 23 June 1959 view. *W. Potter*

*Above:*
Another small Prairie, No 4552, is seen arriving at Looe with the branch goods on 18 July 1960, comprising just two mineral wagons and a van. This is a particularly good view of the L&LR station building with all the paraphernalia of a busy rural station. Note that the name is spelled out in stone-bordered flower beds on the lawn. The Liskeard & Looe Railway operated the branch with four-wheel coaches and a delightful 2-4-0T named *Lady Margaret* which lasted in traffic until well after the GWR took over the branch. *R. C. Riley*

*Left:*
Today, Marsh Mills is the site of the Plym Valley Railway preservation scheme, but the remaining single track is a far cry from this scene of 30 years ago when the first '64xx' 0-6-0PT, No 6400, had just delivered a number of ladies and children on the 4.30pm Plymouth-Tavistock on 29 August 1961. The train is heading away from the camera, running wrong line as the nearer platform had already been taken out of use. The uniformed man relaxing in the rear cab is apparently the Guard, and as the train moves away the passengers can cross safely behind it as there was no footbridge here. The two auto-trailers are of the 1951 design and earlier push-pull vehicles were becoming scarce by this time. *R. C. Riley*

*Above:*
At Moorswater, foot of the climb up to Liskeard, the Looe branch made end-on connection with the remains of the Liskeard and Caradon system, part of which was retained to serve a ball clay pit. Here, in the shadow of the spectacular Moorswater viaduct, stood Moorswater shed, motive power headquarters of the two little systems and latterly a sub-shed of 83E, St Blazey. No 4552 is waiting with the ball clay train before continuing down the branch to Looe to collect any additional traffic. Hidden behind the brake van is the legendary Moorswater 'loo', contrived from an old L&C locomotive firebox positioned over a small stream to provide the most basic of conveniences. *R. C. Riley*

W 6978 W

*Left:*
Bodmin, county town of Cornwall, was served by both the Great Western and the London & South Western with separate terminus stations, while the GWR main line provided a third station three miles away at Bodmin Road. From here the GWR branch curved away to its terminus at Bodmin General, from which another branch diverged to Boscarne Junction and thence to Padstow via the LSWR line. Beeching eliminated both branches into Bodmin but the GWR line survived a while longer for china clay traffic and has become the subject of a preservation project based in Bodmin General station. Sadly, although the Great Western Society had a base here for a while, the little signalbox seen in this view of Bodmin General station was not saved from demolition. Perhaps the preservation group will rebuild it. Green-liveried '45xx' small Prairie No 4569 is seen with the 3.24pm Wadebridge-Bodmin Road service, which involved reversal at Bodmin General, on Whit Monday, 18 May 1959. *M. Mensing*

*Above:*
Several Cornish branches owed their existence to china clay, but none more so than the principle china clay port of Fowey, served by branches from Lostwithiel and Par. The latter lost its passenger service in 1929 but remained for china clay traffic until the 1960s when much of it was converted to a road for the same purpose. The Lostwithiel line served the transhipment wharves at Carne Point and was closed to passengers in January 1965, because the sparse and uneconomic passenger service caused difficulties for the flow of china clay traffic. Fowey was thus a through station where the two branches joined end-on, and here, '14xx' 0-4-2T No 1419 has arrived from Lostwithiel with the passenger service on 4 July 1960. '57xx' 0-6-0PT No 8733 is approaching from Carne Point with a 20ton 'Toad' brake van bound for St Blazey. Note the check-railed, concrete-sleepered track. *W. Potter*

*Above:*
Some evidence of the complexity of working Fowey station is evident in this view taken a few minutes later. No 1419 has reversed its train into the bay platform for stabling so that the main through line is clear for freight traffic. However, it will not be able to depart directly from the bay and will have to reverse into the main platform to head for Lostwithiel. In this view the station, signalbox and goods shed can all be seen, while it also offers a splendid view of the black-painted 'Grampus' ballast wagons, many of which survived in traffic into the 1990s. The Fowey branch is today truncated at Carne Point and the site seen here is a car park. *W. Potter*

*Right:*
Just like the surviving Cornish branches to Looe and St Ives, the Truro-Falmouth branch has seen a fair amount of rationalisation, though it, too, survives. With intermediate stations at Perranwell and Penrhyn to serve, the 9.05am Truro-Falmouth calls at Penmere Platform on Whit Monday 18 May 1959. The train is absolutely typical of the Cornish branches, ex-GWR non-corridor stock headed by a '4575' class 2-6-2T, No 5537. The distinction between 'halts' and 'platforms' was never very clear and certainly Penmere seems to have possessed all the attributes of a classic halt. *M. Mensing*

5537

*Below:*
'45xx' 2-6-2T No 4574 waits in Falmouth sidings as a '4575' 2-6-2T, the version with enlarged, sloping tanks, arrives with the 5.15pm service from Truro. The passenger train is formed of a Collett-era 'B-set', a pair of permanently close-coupled suburban brake composite coaches, built by the GWR specifically for those branch services on which a single-car auto-train would not suffice. The fireman leans from the cab with the single line token clipped into its hoop, ready to drop it off onto the white collecting post opposite the signalbox. The single line electric token system was the standard means of safe operation on all GWR single track branches except those where traffic was so light that a one engine in steam system with a wooden train staff was employed. *M. Mensing*

*Right*
As a busy port, fishing harbour, and ship repair centre, Falmouth generated plenty of freight traffic for the railway. The ubiquitous small 2-6-2Ts were the mainstay of both freight and passenger services in the final years of steam. No 5533 has cleared the main line and No 4574, the last of the original straight-tanked version, is then able to draw its train, including an insulated container out of the sidings at Falmouth station on 14 May 1959. *M. Mensing*

# West Midlands branches

*Left:*
It is all too easy to be captivated by picturesque rural branch lines and to forget that the Great Western branch line had a role in urban areas, too. Though the Greenford loop was probably the only truly urban branch in the London area of the WR, the West Midlands and South Wales could offer a number of lines with an urban backdrop. Darby End halt on the line from Dudley to Old Hill, in the Black Country, was a postwar structure of concrete and corrugated iron, its rudimentary shelters scarcely offering much incentive to the intending traveller. Push-pull fitted '64xx' 0-6-0PT No 6434 is seen departing with the 7.00pm Old Hill-Dudley on 14 May 1964. The auto-trailer is a converted brake carriage and this West Midlands suburban service was a victim of the Beeching axe. *M. Mensing*

*Right:*
This busy scene at Old Hill on 14 May 1964 is even busier than it at first appears. '51xx' 2-6-2T No 4172 is banking the rear of a freight from Wolverhampton off the Windmill End branch with BR Standard '9F' 2-10-0 No 92118 at the front. Gloucester single unit railcar No W55004 is waiting on the branch, between workings to Dudley. This scene typifies the period with steam and diesel alongside. The railcar is in original light green livery with 'whiskers' on the ends, while the condition of the Prairie and the brake van are perfect guides for weathering models. No W55004 passed eventually to the LMR and in the 1980s was one of two vehicles used to re-introduce services between Kettering and Corby. These were withdrawn when the local authority ceased its financial support in a bid to cut its Community Charge. Railcars Nos 55004/11 were noted dumped at Tyseley in summer 1990, awaiting withdrawal. *M. Mensing*

B2
NOT
COMMON USE

*Left:*
The North Warwickshire line from Tyseley through Henley-in-Arden to Stratford-upon-Avon was built around the turn of the century with standard GWR structures of the period. Yardley Wood station, seen here with its red brick buildings and narrow canopies, was typical. Though they originally had a rural aspect, most of the line's dozen or so stations have seen much surrounding development in recent years. On Sunday 3 May 1964, Collett '2251' 0-6-0 No 3217 had charge of a permanent way train engaged in work at the station and is drawing slowly forward. The black carriage in the centre has a most interesting history, having been built as Pharmacy Car No 39036 and used abroad in World War 1 ambulance trains. In 1921 it was converted to a milk train brake, No 1400, and was transferred to Departmental use as a Mess Van in February 1948, becoming No 14060. It is now preserved on the Severn Valley Railway. *M. Mensing*

*Above:*
The Presteigne branch engine, '14xx' 0-4-2T No 1420 is the subject of this excellent portrait taken at Leominster shed in 1959. The locomotive is in its final form, with top-feed and painted in fully-lined passenger livery with the 1958 BR totem. It is clean and smart, with all its plates still in place. Despite its comparatively modern appearance, the shed is gas lit and is playing host only to a couple of mineral wagons. *A. Sainty collection/Colour-Rail*

5167
MUCH WENLOCK

*Left:*
The cross-country route from Wellington-Craven Arms was a fascinating route through the area that gave birth to the industrial revolution, crossing the Severn Valley at Buildwas and climbing to Much Wenlock before setting out through rural Shropshire. The Much Wenlock-Craven Arms section lost its passenger service in 1951 but was retained as far as Longville for occasional agricultural traffic. Much Wenlock was served from Wellington with a mixture of steam-hauled workings and single Gloucester RC&W railcars. '44xx' 2-6-2Ts were favourites for the lightly laid stretch beyond Wenlock, but when services were cut back, the larger Prairie tanks could be used. Arguably the most attractive of all WR branch stations, Much Wenlock was host to '41xx' 2-6-2T No 5167, seen after arrival from Wellington, on 31 August 1959.
*Frank Hornby/Colour-Rail*

*Above:*
In the early 1960s my brother and I built a model of the Much Wenlock branch. Eager to build the junction station, where the branch crossed the now famous Severn Valley line, we visited Buildwas, which was then accessible only by bus. Alas we were too late and the whole station site had vanished under construction work for Ironbridge 'B' power station. That I never saw this curious arrangement with the Wenlock branch platform above and behind the Severn Valley ones, is a source of great regret. On 6 September 1963, Gloucester single railcar No W55005, from the class which replaced the Great Western railcars on this route, pauses at Buildwas with the 2.05pm Kidderminster-Shrewsbury. The huge and informative station nameboard was typical of GWR junctions, though by this time Buildwas had ceased to be a junction for passenger services. *Hugh Ballantyne*

*Above:*
The Great Western's AEC diesel railcars were never very many in number, but were highly successful and most lasted in traffic for over 20 years. The later style vehicles, from No 19 onwards, were concentrated in the Worcester area for their final couple of years, having been ousted from London area branches by new Gloucester RC&W-built cars. They were regular performers on the Bromyard and Cleobury Mortimer branches and on the Severn Valley line from Shrewsbury to Hartlebury. At the latter station, green-liveried car No W23W has arrived from Shrewsbury, and is glimpsed through the rear cab window of sister, No W24W as it departs. Not all the railcars received the final green livery, several of the angular cars and all the earlier streamlined vehicles, going for scrap in carmine and cream. Cars Nos 4/20 and 22 survive in preservation. *Michael Farr*

# Welsh branches

*Above:*
In Wales, particularly South Wales, the GWR inherited many lines at the Grouping in 1923, and the distinction between branches, through routes and main lines becomes blurred by the sheer complexity of the railway system in the South Wales valleys. The character of many of these lines was quite unlike anywhere else on the GWR and the method of operation required a different approach to motive power. The valley lines were operated with locomotives running chimney-first uphill and the 0-6-2T wheel arrangement had been found by the pre-Grouping companies to be ideal for bunker-first downhill running. The GWR supplemented or replaced these earlier designs with its own new standard 0-6-2T designed by Collett, the '56xx' class. No 5622 of this type is seen running light through Hengoed Low Level, the former Rhymney Railway station, seen from the Great Western's own High Level station. Note the GWR gaslamps and fencing, and BR signs. imposed on a distinctly non-Great Western station with a curved footbridge reminiscent of Midland Railway style. The date was 3 June 1961. *Peter W. Gray*

*Above:*
Many of the South Wales branches possessed a fascinating mixture of rural, urban and industrial hinterland. At Neath Riverside on 20 August 1962, the 3.00pm service from Colbren Junction arrives at 3.43pm behind a '57xx' 0-6-0PT, amid just such a mixture. Against a backdrop of wooded hills the station presents a dilapidated industrial scene with tatty buildings and a much-rationalised station. One platform is out of use, while the other has a patchwork surface and the most rudimentary of shelters dating from late GWR or early BR days. Piles of signalling equipment abound, and an Engineers' Department mess van in black livery is stabled in the bay. There were comparatively few auto-train workings in South Wales, with heavier services worked by 0-6-2Ts and Prairies, and lighter ones such as this in the hands of 0-6-0PTs. The Hawksworth brake second, downgraded to branchline work, adds interest to this scene. Services from Neath Riverside to Swansea had ceased in 1936, and those to Brecon finished just two months after this photograph was taken. *Peter W. Gray*

*Right:*
Brecon was approached from the west by the Neath and Brecon line, and from the east by the Brecon & Merthyr over which services also operated from Hereford and from Moat Lane Junction. All served primarily rural areas and services from Neath ceased in October 1962, all the others being discontinued from 31 December 1962 to leave the county town without rail service. The station building, as seen here on 20 August 1962, was distinctive and this delightfully busy view shows it well. A Morris Minor Post Office van and a Ford Prefect van in the fashionable 'salmon' pink of the day await traffic from the 4.00pm Hereford service which has just arrived behind Ivatt '2MT' 2-6-0 No 46513. Though an LMS design, these locomotives migrated to a number of GWR routes after Nationalisation, and were regularly seen on services from Moat Lane and Hereford to Brecon. On the left, '57xx' No 3768 waits with the 6.20pm departure for Neath Riverside. *Peter W. Gray*

BRECON
46513

*Above:*
Strata Florida was the unlikely-sounding name of a remote and desolate station in the heart of Cardiganshire on the Aberystwyth-Carmarthen line built by the equally unlikely Manchester & Milford Railway, which served neither place in its title. A southbound train is arriving behind '43xx' 2-6-0 No 6375, a class whose coverage in this volume has been rather less than its widespread use might have warranted, and crossing an Aberystwyth-bound train. This quick shot from the carriage window has earned its place in this volume by catching a number of excellent station details. To the right is a hand-crane of about 3ton capacity, while the platform carries a standard GWR water column complete with fire devil to prevent it freezing in winter. The structure behind it, still finished in GWR 'dark stone' paint, is a cast iron urinal. These were particularly rare by this time and luckily one or two have found their way into preservation. This example, owing to its exposed (!) location, has had a timber roof added – usually they were open. *Colour-Rail*

*Right:*
Bala Junction, at the head of Bala Lake, on the Ruabon-Barmouth line, was junction for the Blaenau Ffestiniog branch. It was unusual in having virtually no public access, just a footpath across the fields, as it served no local community. By 25 April 1964, when this view was taken, the original GWR nameboard had been altered to reflect the termination of the branch service at Bala. The main platform was an island, with a third platform nearer the camera, having a 'pagoda' waiting shed whose roof can just be seen. The signal is just coming off for a very grimy BR standard '2MT' 2-6-2T to depart with the one-coach branch train. By this time former GWR lines in north and west Wales had passed to the control of London Midland Region, who withdrew all services on the Ruabon-Barmouth line and the Bala branch from January 1965, although the Llangollen-Ruabon section had been severed by flooding a few weeks earlier. *G. Lumb*

BALA JUNCTION
CHANGE FOR
BALA

*Above:*
The ex-GWR lines in the northwest passed to LMR control with regional boundary changes under Beeching, and a number of GWR locomotive depots changed hands. Birkenhead-based '57xx' 0-6-0PT No 9630 wears a 6C shedplate as it shunts the goods from Ruabon at Trevor on 25 July 1966. By this time overhead electrification warning signs were being plastered on steam locomotives which might venture under the wires of the West Coast electrification, while original name and numberplates were disappearing equally fast. No 9630 has only a crude painted number to identify it, but otherwise looks the part at the head of a typical branch freight in the twilight months of the breed. Another concession to LMR control in this otherwise perfect branch freight train is the substitution of an ex-LMS vacuum-fitted brake van for the usual 'Toad'. *M. H. Yardley*

*Right:*
A number of '57xx' 0-6-0PTs were kept on by the LMR to service branch freight in the West Midlands and in the northwest around Wrexham well after steam working on the WR had ceased. Another tatty Birkenhead-based example, No 9610, is here seen shunting King's Mills siding, Wrexham, on the remains of the former Cambrian branch through Bangor-on-Dee to Ellesmere. The traffic is in sheeted, vacuum-fitted open wagons. No 9610 has also lost all its plates and was destined to be one of the last of its type in traffic. The date of this view, when wagonload traffic was still being usefully conveyed by rail, was 25 July 1966. *M. H. Yardley*

*Below:*
Another late survivor of its class thanks to the LMR was small-wheeled '16xx' 0-6-0PT No 1628. On 1 June 1966 it was hurrying away from Cadbury's Bangor-on-Dee factory with two empty open wagons and a BR 20ton brake van. the '16xx' class was introduced in 1949 for light branch goods and shunting work and No 1628 was a mere teenager when scrapped a few months after this picture was taken. *M. H. Yardley*

# Dean and Wye branches

*Below:*
If the Severn Valley line had not been preserved, the Gloucester-Ross-Hereford line would have been an obvious choice. Though it linked two cities, it served only Ross and a handful of villages in between, and Ross lost much of its railway significance when the branch to Monmouth closed. One of my first railway photographs was taken from exactly this location, though sadly on a Sunday with no trains present. Few of the lines illustrated in this volume would have boasted a Sunday service under BR. The 2.43pm Hereford-Gloucester has '43xx' 2-6-0 No 7319 surrounded by birdsong and an intrusive insect as it passes Weston-under-Penyard halt on 15 May 1964. *M. Mensing*

*Above:*
The town of Monmouth was served by rural lines from Pontypool Road, Chepstow and Ross-on-Wye, but none offered much traffic potential. The service to Pontypool Road had ceased in 1955 and the others were to end from 5 January 1959. As seen here, the service from Ross was normally an autotrain worked by a '14xx' 0-4-2T which was shedded at Ross. On 28 May 1958 No 1455, a grubby black-liveried example, was working the service with W237W, an unlined 1951 autotrailer. The vehicle's bus-type seats and pastel interior panels can be clearly seen, as can the driver. Like many rural station buildings, that at Monmouth Troy served other uses after its closure and was later acquired by the Gloucestershire Warwickshire Railway. The stone building was dismantled and moved piece by piece to Winchcombe, where it will be re-erected on the preserved stretch of the ex-GWR Cheltenham-Honeybourne line. *T. B. Owen*

*Right:*
It is well-known that from the mid-1950s the BR Board began to allow the Regions a degree of autonomy which had been resisted following Nationalisation in 1948. On the WR this slight relaxation caused a return to chocolate and cream livery for Mk1 coaching stock and to Swindon green livery for passenger and mixed traffic locomotives. This extended to embrace even the smallest passenger tanks which were given the same full lining as express passenger classes, a privilege they had never enjoyed in GWR days. Perhaps the ultimate in overdoing it, was the application of full lining to '64xx' class 0-6-0PT autotanks, such as No 6431, seen here in a delightful scene at Monmouth Troy. As the Chepstow train waits to depart, the driver tops up the tanks, while the fireman washes his tea cup ready for the important business of the day. The branch can be seen curving away to the right over the viaduct. The preserved Dart Valley Railway acquired '64xx' tanks for preservation but 6431 was not one of the lucky ones. *T. B. Owen*

6431

*Left:*
The Forest of Dean contained a wealth of railway interest, for mining and industrial development had led to numerous lines, some of them only ever used for freight traffic. The two main promoters were the GWR and the Severn & Wye Railway, the latter's most well-known feature being the Severn Bridge which took it across to Berkeley Road to link up with its friendly neighbour, the Midland Railway. The lines all eventually passed to its much less friendly neighbour, the GWR. At Bilson Junction the Severn & Wye line to Cinderford made connection with the GWR's line from Bullo Pill to Drybrook and it was here that trains were marshalled in the small yard for onward movement. By the 1960s the WR was operating all the remaining lines in the Forest for freight only, and Bilson remained a focal point on the system. On 22 September 1965, '57xx' 0-6-0PT No 4689 is heading south from Bilson Junction with empty tank wagons. The standard GWR timber signalbox is finished in the brown and cream colour scheme used by the Western Region and so often thought to be GWR colours. *W. Potter*

*Right:*
The GWR had a number of ballast quarries in the area, that at Tintern being the largest and best-known. Tintern lasted until all ballast quarrying for the Region was centred on the former Southern Railway quarry at Meldon, but Whitecliff survived with rail connection until 1967, after which the stone was moved by road to Parkend until that, too, closed in 1976. At 12.15pm on 16 August 1965, another of the '57xx' Panniers which monopolised the Forest freight services, No 4698, brings a train of 'dogfish' ballast wagons from Whitecliff quarry up the branch towards Coleford. The 24ton 'dogfish' was a BR design of which more than 1,200 were built. They were popular with the permanent way department because three sets of independent hopper doors allowed the ballast to be dumped to either side or in the centre of the track. *W. Potter*

*Left:*
This is another view which is included in order to show the GWR branch line in its true rural setting. The scars of abandoned quarrying scarcely mar the backdrop of Fetter Hill as No 4698 makes its way towards Coleford with a goods working of three open wagons and a van. The time was 1.50pm on 16 August 1967 and nothing but the sound of the train disturbs the peace of this pleasant spot. *W. Potter*

*Above:*
On 13 May 1961 the Stephenson Locomotive Society ran a tour of the Forest lines with auto-fitted 0-6-0PT No 6437 sandwiched between three of the 1951-built trailers. The formation was made most unusual by the addition of '57xx' 0-6-0PT No 8701, which was not auto-fitted and was presumably there to provide assistance on the steep gradients. With No 8701 leading, the well-laden tour is seen making its way between Parkend and Coleford Junction on the former Severn & Wye main line. The check-railed curve indicates how the Forest lines twisted around the hillsides and suggest that perhaps push-pull operation might have been impractical because of problems with the linkage on sharp curves. *W. Potter*

*Above:*
What a marvellous scene is this model-like view at Parkend, with almost too much detail to take in. The wagons in the foreground are standing in the former Parkend station area, while the Forest engine No 4698 is propelling a wagon round towards Marsh sidings (Parkend goods). Note the proximity of the two hand-operated level crossings, and the number of staff necessary for one wagon movement. The road vehicles beyond the rustic bus shelter include a Commer milk float, pick-up truck and a Ferguson tractor. *W. Potter*

*Right:*
Soudley No 1, or Lower Soudley, crossing was one of the most photogenic spots on the GWR line from Bullo Pill up to Cinderford. The SLS special of 13 May 1961 is seen again, heading away from the camera, having just emerged from the 1,065yd Haie Hill tunnel on the right. The little crossing with its ground frame and classically drooping distant signal complete as near perfect a branch line picture as it is possible to find. *W. Potter*

*Left:*
'57xx' 0-6-0PT No 8701 appears again, this time with the goods from Bullo Pill emerging from Bradley Hill tunnel and over the tiny crossing at Upper Soudley. If the headlamp is correct and the locomotive is approaching the photographer, then the distant signal is giving a conflicting indication! The Pannier appears to have some steam leaks and is possibly having trouble with damp rails in this 12 October 1960 view. *B. J. Ashworth*

*Back cover:*
Flowers in the garden and girls on roller skates add to the charm of Newent station as the 12.10pm Gloucester Central-Ledbury waits for departure time on Saturday 20 June 1959. The line closed three weeks later. '45xx' class 2-6-2T No 4573 provides the motive power, although the working timetable showed the train as 'diesel'. *J. Tawse*